WORKBOOK

For

FERVENT

A Woman's Battle Plan To Serious, Specific and Strategic Prayer

A Guide To Priscilla Shirer's Book

Willow Reads

This workbook is intended to be a companion to the original book - Fervent: A Woman's Battle Plan to Serious, Specific and Strategic Prayer by Priscilla Shirer, and is designed to complement the lessons and content presented in the original work.

It is not meant to replace or substitute for the original book. While this workbook provides exercises, activities, and additional material to enhance your understanding and application of the original book's concepts, it is best used in conjunction with the reading of the original book.

The author and publisher of this workbook make no representations or warranties regarding the accuracy or completeness of the content in the original book. This workbook is provided "as is" and is meant for informational and educational purposes only.

How To Use This Workbook

This workbook is designed to help you engage with the content of the original book in a meaningful and interactive way.

1. Start with the Overview
Begin your journey through this workbook by reading the "Overview of the Original Book." This section provides a concise summary of the key themes and concepts explored in the main book. It's the perfect starting point to refresh your memory or get acquainted with the book's content.

2. Dive into the Chapters
Each chapter in this workbook is dedicated to a corresponding chapter in the original book. Here's what you'll find in each chapter section:

Key Lessons:
Discover the fundamental takeaways from the main book's chapter. These key lessons will help you understand the core concepts discussed in that section.

Exercises:
Engage actively with the material through exercises that encourage reflection, application, and critical thinking.

These exercises will help you internalize and apply the book's teachings.

Questions:
Explore thought-provoking questions related to the chapter's content. Use these questions for personal reflection or as a basis for discussions with others who have read the original book.

Chapter Summary:
Get a quick recap of the chapter's main points. This summary will reinforce your understanding and serve as a handy reference.

3. Final Evaluation Questions
Towards the end of this workbook, you'll find a section titled "Final Evaluation Questions." This is your opportunity to test your knowledge and insights gained from the entire book. These questions will challenge you to think critically, make connections, and draw your own conclusions.

4. Your Journey, Your Pace
This workbook is designed to be flexible. You can use it in a way that suits your needs and preferences. Whether you want to complete it in a linear fashion, jump to specific chapters, or revisit sections for further reflection, it's entirely up to you.

Overview Of The Original Book

In her book "Fervent: A Woman's Battle Plan to Serious, Specific and Strategic Prayer," Priscilla Shirer presents a compelling and practical guide to prayer, encouraging women to deepen their spiritual lives and engage in powerful, effective communication with God. She emphasizes the importance of fervent prayer, characterized by passion, intensity, and unwavering focus, as a weapon against spiritual warfare and a means of transforming personal challenges and interceding for others.

Shirer begins by establishing the foundation for fervent prayer, reminding readers of God's desire to hear and respond to their prayers. She dispels common misconceptions about prayer, encouraging women to view it not as a mere ritual or obligation but as a powerful tool for spiritual growth and personal transformation.

Throughout the book, she outlines specific strategies for crafting effective prayers, emphasizing the importance of clarity, specificity, and alignment with God's will. She encourages women to identify specific areas of their lives, relationships, and the world around them that need God's intervention and to pray with unwavering faith and determination.

Shirer also delves into the importance of spiritual warfare prayer, recognizing that the world is filled with unseen forces that can hinder God's work and bring harm to individuals and communities. She provides guidance on identifying and confronting these spiritual enemies through prayer, emphasizing the power of God's word and the authority of Jesus Christ.

In addition to individual prayer, Shirer highlights the significance of corporate prayer, encouraging women to unite with other believers to intercede for their families, churches, communities, and the world. She emphasizes the power of collective prayer and the synergistic effect of believers coming together in unity to seek God's intervention.

Throughout the book, Shirer interweaves personal anecdotes and biblical examples to illustrate the transformative power of fervent prayer. She shares stories of individuals and communities whose lives have been radically impacted through persistent, focused prayer, demonstrating the practical impact of this spiritual weapon.

Shirer encourages women to embrace fervent prayer as a lifelong practice, not just as a temporary response to crisis or difficulty.

Your Passion

Chapter Summary

This chapter emphasizes the crucial role of passion in fervent prayer, highlighting its ability to fuel effective communication with God and ignite spiritual transformation. The author explains that passion in prayer is not merely about feeling strong emotions but about aligning one's heart and mind with God's desires and purposes.

She begins by defining passion as an intense enthusiasm or eagerness for something, emphasizing that it is a powerful motivator that can drive individuals to take action and achieve their goals. She argues that this same level of passion can and should be applied to prayer, as it is the lifeblood of effective communication with God.

Shirer identifies several key elements of passionate prayer:

Intensity: Passionate prayer is not passive or indifferent but characterized by fervor, zeal, and a deep desire to connect with God.

Focus: Passionate prayer is not scattered or distracted but focused on specific needs, concerns, and desires, seeking God's guidance and intervention.

Authenticity: Passionate prayer is not about putting on a show or conforming to expectations but about expressing one's true heart and emotions before God.

Persistence: Passionate prayer is not about giving up easily but about persevering in prayer, believing in God's promises, and trusting in His timing.

She emphasizes that passion in prayer is not a natural human tendency but a gift from the Holy Spirit. She encourages women to seek the Spirit's empowerment to ignite their prayer lives and experience the transformative power of fervent prayer.

To foster passion in prayer, she suggests several practical steps:

1. Identifying God's passions: Studying the Bible and seeking God's revelation can help individuals discover the things that matter deeply to Him, aligning their own passions with His.

2. Connecting with God's heart: Spending time in worship, meditation, and reflection can cultivate

a deeper understanding of God's character and His love for humanity.

3. Praying with a vision: Visualizing the desired outcome of prayers can fuel passion and determination, keeping the focus on God's promises and purposes.

4. Praying with urgency: Recognizing the importance and urgency of prayer can motivate individuals to approach God with passion and intensity.

Key Lessons

Passion is the Lifeblood of Fervent Prayer: Passion is not just an emotion; it's a driving force that fuels effective communication with God. Passionate prayer is characterized by intensity, focus, authenticity, and persistence.

Passionate Prayer Aligns with God's Desires: Passion in prayer is not about seeking personal fulfillment or immediate gratification; it's about aligning one's heart and mind with God's desires and purposes. It's about bringing God's passions to life through our prayers.

Passion in Prayer is a Gift from the Holy Spirit: The ability to pray with passion is not a natural human tendency but a gift from the Holy Spirit. Seek the Spirit's empowerment to ignite your prayer life and experience the transformative power of fervent prayer.

Cultivating Passion in Prayer Requires Intentionality: Passion in prayer doesn't happen by accident; it requires intentionality and effort. Practice identifying God's passions, connecting with His heart, praying with a vision, and approaching prayer with urgency.

Self-reflection questions

Have you actively sought to align your prayers with God's desires and purposes, considering passion as the driving force behind effective communication with Him?

_____

_____

_____

_____

_____

_____

_____

In your prayer life, do you exhibit the intensity characterized by fervor, zeal, and a deep desire to connect with God, as emphasized in the discussion of passionate prayer?

_____

_____

_____

_____

_____

_____

_____

_____

How well are you maintaining focus in your prayers, ensuring they are not scattered or distracted but specifically directed toward your needs, concerns, and desires, seeking God's guidance and intervention?

_____

_____

_____

_____

_____

_____

Reflect on the authenticity of your prayer life. Are you genuine in expressing your true heart and emotions before God, or do you find yourself conforming to expectations or putting on a show?

_____

_____

_____

_____

_____

_____

_____

_____

Consider your persistence in prayer. Are you persevering, believing in God's promises, and trusting in His timing, or do you tend to give up easily?

_____

_____

_____

_____

_____

_____

_____

Life-Changing Exercises

1. Take a moment each day to assess the intensity of your prayers. Ask yourself if your prayers reflect fervor, zeal, and a genuine desire to connect with God.

2. Create a prayer journal specifically dedicated to your needs, concerns, and desires. Ensure that each entry is focused and seeks God's guidance and intervention in those specific areas.

3. Make a conscious effort to express your true emotions before God without holding back. Avoid putting on a show or conforming to expectations in your prayer life.

4. Set a goal to persevere in prayer for a specific duration, perhaps a week or a month. Embrace the challenge of believing in God's promises and trusting in His timing, even when faced with difficulties.

Your Focus

Chapter Summary

This chapter emphasizes the crucial role of focus in fervent prayer, highlighting its ability to filter out distractions, align intentions, and enhance the power of communication with God. The author explains that focused prayer is not about multitasking or achieving a certain level of spiritual enlightenment but about intentionally directing one's heart and mind towards God, seeking His presence and guidance.

The chapter begins by acknowledging the challenges of maintaining focus in prayer, recognizing the constant barrage of distractions and competing demands that can pull individuals away from genuine connection with God. The author emphasizes that focused prayer is not about emptying one's mind or achieving a state of perfect stillness but about cultivating a sense of awareness and intentionality in the presence of God.

She identifies several key aspects of focused prayer:

Clarity of purpose: Before entering prayer, it is essential to have a clear understanding of what one wants to pray for. This clarity will help maintain focus and avoid aimless or wandering prayers.

Conscious engagement: Focused prayer requires conscious engagement with God, actively listening for His voice and responding to His promptings. This engagement goes beyond mere repetition of words or formulas.

Eliminating distractions: To cultivate focus, it is essential to identify and eliminate distractions, whether internal or external. This may involve finding a quiet place, silencing notifications, and engaging in calming practices before prayer.

Persevering in focus: Maintaining focus in prayer requires perseverance and discipline, especially in the face of distractions and mental fatigue. It is important to gently bring the mind back to God when it wanders.

She emphasizes that focused prayer is not about achieving a perfect state of concentration but about maintaining a consistent orientation towards God throughout the prayer. She encourages women to view their prayer lives as a journey of spiritual growth, where focus deepens over time through practice and reliance on the Holy Spirit.

To enhance focus in prayer, several practical steps are suggested:

1. Developing a prayer routine: Establishing a regular time and place for prayer can help create a sense of structure and expectation, making it easier to settle into focused prayer.

2. Using prayer guides: Prayer guides or prompts can provide a framework for prayers, helping to maintain focus and preventing wandering thoughts.

3. Engaging the senses: Incorporating elements of sight, sound, or smell can enhance focus and create a more immersive prayer experience.

4. Seeking the Holy Spirit's guidance: The Holy Spirit can help individuals identify distractions, overcome mental fatigue, and maintain focus throughout prayer.

Key Lessons

Focus is Crucial for Effective Prayer: Focused prayer is not about achieving a certain level of spiritual enlightenment or multitasking; it's about intentionally directing one's heart and mind towards God, seeking His presence and guidance.

Clarity of Purpose Precedes Focused Prayer: Before entering prayer, it's essential to have a clear understanding of what one wants to pray for. This clarity will help maintain focus and avoid aimless or wandering prayers.

Conscious Engagement Enhances Prayerful Communication: Focused prayer requires conscious engagement with God, actively listening for His voice and responding to His promptings. It's not merely about repetition of words or formulas.

Eliminating Distractions Fosters a Deeper Connection with God: To cultivate focus, it's essential to identify and eliminate distractions, both internal and external. This may involve finding a quiet place, silencing notifications, and engaging in calming practices before prayer.

Persevering in Focus Strengthens Spiritual Connection: Maintaining focus in prayer requires perseverance and discipline, especially in the face of distractions and mental fatigue. Gently bring the mind back to God when it wanders.

Self-reflection questions

Before your next prayer, reflect on whether you have a clear understanding of what you want to pray for. Are your intentions well-defined, contributing to a focused and purposeful prayer?

Assess your engagement with God in recent prayers. Are you actively listening for His voice and responding to His promptings, or have your prayers become a routine of words without genuine connection?

Take a moment to identify potential distractions, both internal and external, that may hinder your focused prayer. What steps can you take to eliminate or minimize these distractions before entering into prayer?

_____

_____

_____

_____

_____

_____

_____

_____

_____

Reflect on your recent prayer experiences. How well have you persevered in maintaining focus, especially when faced with distractions and mental fatigue? Consider strategies to gently bring your mind back to God.

Consider viewing your prayer life as a journey of spiritual growth. How has your focus in prayer evolved over time, and what practices have contributed to this deepening connection with God?

_____

_____

_____

_____

_____

_____

_____

_____

Evaluate your prayer routine. Have you established a regular time and place for prayer to create structure and expectation? If not, how can you incorporate this into your daily life?

_____

_____

_____

_____

_____

_____

_____

Life-Changing Exercises

1. Take dedicated time to clarify your prayer intentions before entering prayer. Write down what you want to pray for, ensuring a clear purpose to maintain focus and avoid aimless wandering during your prayer time.

2. Challenge yourself to actively engage with God during prayer. Instead of relying on rote words or formulas, consciously listen for His voice and respond to His promptings, fostering a deeper and more meaningful connection.

3. Conduct a "distraction detox" before your next prayer session. Find a quiet place, silence notifications, and engage in calming practices to eliminate external and internal distractions, creating an environment conducive to focused prayer.

4. Set a goal for maintaining focus in prayer. Practice perseverance and discipline, gently bringing your mind back to God when distractions or mental fatigue arise. Track your progress over time to witness the development of your focus.

Your Identity

Chapter Summary

In this section, the author explains that a clear understanding of one's identity as a child of God, forgiven and loved unconditionally, empowers individuals to approach God with confidence and boldness, knowing that they are welcomed and valued in His presence.

The author begins by highlighting the prevalent issue of identity confusion in today's world, where individuals often seek their worth and value in external factors such as appearance, achievements, or social status. This pursuit of external validation can lead to feelings of insecurity, inadequacy, and a sense of disconnection from God's true purpose for their lives.

In contrast, she presents the liberating truth of one's identity in Christ, emphasizing that it is not defined by external circumstances or personal shortcomings but by God's unchanging love and acceptance. As children of God, individuals are forgiven, redeemed, and deeply loved, regardless of their past mistakes or perceived flaws.

The author identifies several key aspects of one's identity in Christ:

Beloved Child of God: Every individual is a unique and cherished child of God, created in His image and bearing His divine spark. This identity is not earned or deserved but freely given by God's grace.

Forgiven and Redeemed: Through the sacrificial death of Jesus Christ, individuals are forgiven of their sins and reconciled to God. This forgiveness is not conditional on self-improvement or perfect performance but is a gift from God's immense love.

Valued and Empowered: God has a unique purpose and plan for each individual, and He has equipped them with the gifts and abilities to fulfill that purpose.

Secure and Empowered: Rooted in God's love and acceptance, individuals can approach prayer with confidence and boldness, knowing that they are heard and valued by their heavenly Father.

This chapter emphasizes that understanding and embracing one's identity in Christ is not a static one-time event but an ongoing journey of spiritual growth. As individuals deepen their understanding of God's love and acceptance, they experience a transformation in their self-perception and their relationship with God.

Key Lessons

True Identity Lies in Christ, Not External Factors: One's true identity is not defined by external factors such as appearance, achievements, or social status. Instead, it is rooted in one's relationship with God as a beloved child, forgiven and redeemed through Jesus Christ.

God's Love and Acceptance Provide Unwavering Foundation: God's love and acceptance are not conditional on self-improvement or perfect performance. They are freely given gifts that provide a secure and unwavering foundation for one's identity.

Understanding Identity in Christ Empowers Fervent Prayer: Recognizing one's identity as a child of God empowers individuals to approach prayer with confidence, boldness, and a sense of belonging in God's presence.

Embracing Identity in Christ is an Ongoing Journey: Deepening one's understanding of their identity in Christ is not a one-time event but an ongoing journey of spiritual growth and transformation.

Cultivating Identity in Christ Requires Intentional Practices: Embracing one's identity in Christ requires intentional practices such as immersing oneself in Scripture, seeking God's revelation, connecting with supportive believers, and challenging negative self-talk.

Self-reflection questions

Have you recently reflected on your identity as a beloved child of God, recognizing that it is not based on external factors but on God's unchanging love and acceptance?

_____

_____

_____

_____

_____

_____

_____

Are you aware of any tendencies to seek your worth or value in external factors, such as appearance or achievements? How might this pursuit impact your sense of connection with God's purpose for your life?

_____

_____

_____

_____

_____

_____

_____

_____

_____

Do you fully embrace the liberating truth that, as a child of God, you are forgiven and redeemed, not based on your efforts but as a gift from God's immense love?

_____

_____

_____

_____

_____

_____

Reflect on your view of yourself as a unique and cherished child of God, created in His image. How does this perspective influence your self-perception and interactions with others?

_____

_____

_____

_____

_____

_____

_____

_____

_____

_____

Are you conscious of God's unique purpose and plan for your life? How do you recognize and utilize the gifts and abilities He has equipped you with to fulfill that purpose?

_____

_____

_____

_____

_____

_____

_____

_____

_____

_____

_____

Consider your approach to prayer. Do you approach God with confidence and boldness, rooted in the secure knowledge that you are heard and valued as His beloved child?

_____

_____

_____

_____

_____

_____

_____

_____

_____

Reflect on your journey of understanding and embracing your identity in Christ. How has this awareness evolved over time, contributing to a transformation in your self-perception and relationship with God?

_____

_____

_____

_____

_____

_____

_____

_____

Life-Changing Exercises

1. Start a journal dedicated to exploring your identity as a beloved child of God. Regularly write about how this understanding shapes your thoughts, actions, and interactions, fostering a deeper connection with God.

2. Identify one external factor (e.g., appearance, achievements) from which you tend to seek validation. Challenge yourself to detach your worth from this factor for a specified period. Reflect on how this shift impacts your sense of connection with God's purpose.

3. Take intentional time to reflect on the concept of forgiveness as a gift from God's immense love. Write down instances where you struggle with self-forgiveness and consciously release these burdens, embracing the freedom of God's forgiveness.

4. Explore and identify your unique gifts and abilities that God has equipped you with for His purpose. Create a plan to actively use these gifts in your daily life, aligning them with God's intended plan for you.

5. Incorporate a new approach to prayer by consciously infusing confidence and boldness. Before each prayer session, remind yourself of your identity as a beloved child of God. Approach your prayers with the assurance that you are heard and valued, fostering a deeper connection with your heavenly Father.

Your Family

Chapter Summary

This chapter explains that prayer is not a mere last resort or a means of micromanaging family affairs but a powerful tool for spiritual warfare and a means of aligning families with God's purpose.

The author begins by acknowledging the challenges and struggles that families face in today's world, from external pressures and distractions to internal conflicts and misunderstandings. These challenges can strain relationships, erode unity, and create a sense of helplessness.

In contrast, the chapter presents prayer as a transformative force that can bring healing, restoration, and protection to families. Through prayer, individuals can:

Seek God's intervention in specific family challenges: Prayer can be directed towards specific issues such as wayward children, strained relationships, or financial difficulties, inviting God's guidance and intervention.

Protect family members from spiritual attack: The author emphasizes the role of prayer in spiritual warfare, recognizing that families are not immune to spiritual forces that can harm and divide.

Strengthen family bonds and unity: Prayer can foster a sense of unity and connection within families, encouraging open communication, forgiveness, and mutual support.

The author identifies several key aspects of fervent prayer for families:

1. Specificity: Prayers for family members should be specific and focused, addressing specific needs, concerns, and desires.

2. Consistency: Consistent prayer for family members creates a spiritual force field around them, providing ongoing protection and guidance.

3. Agreement with other believers: Prayer for family members can be amplified when joined with other believers in a spirit of unity and purpose.

4. Faith and perseverance: Fervent prayer for family requires unwavering faith and perseverance,

believing in God's power to transform even the most challenging situations.

She emphasizes that prayer for family members is not about controlling or manipulating outcomes but about aligning the family with God's will and seeking His intervention in their lives. It is about recognizing God's role as the ultimate authority and surrendering family concerns to His care.

Key Lessons

Prayer is a Powerful Tool for Spiritual Warfare and Restoration: Prayer is not a mere last resort or a means of micromanaging family affairs; it is a powerful tool for spiritual warfare and a means of aligning families with God's purpose.

Fervent Prayer Brings Protection, Healing, and Restoration to Families: Through prayer, individuals can seek God's intervention in specific family challenges, protect family members from spiritual attack, and strengthen family bonds and unity.

Prayer for Family Members Requires Specificity, Consistency, Agreement, and Perseverance: Prayers for family members should be specific, consistent, made in agreement with other believers, and characterized by unwavering faith and perseverance.

Prayer for Family Members is Not About Control but Surrender and Alignment: Fervent prayer for family members is not about controlling or manipulating outcomes; it is about aligning the family with God's will and seeking His intervention in their lives.

Creating a Prayer List, Engaging in Prayer with Other Family Members, and Seeking Guidance from Spiritual Leaders Enhances Prayer for Families: Identifying specific prayer needs, creating a prayer list, praying together as a family, and seeking guidance from spiritual leaders can enhance prayer ministry within the family.

Self-reflection questions

Have you been specific and focused in your prayers for family members, addressing their unique needs, concerns, and desires rather than offering generalized requests?

_____

_____

_____

_____

_____

_____

_____

Reflect on the consistency of your prayers for family members. Are you actively creating a spiritual force field around them through consistent prayer, providing ongoing protection and guidance?

_____

_____

_____

_____

_____

_____

_____

_____

_____

_____

Consider your prayer life in relation to your family. Are you engaging in prayer with other believers in a spirit of unity and purpose, amplifying the impact of your collective prayers for your family?

_____

_____

_____

_____

_____

_____

_____

_____

_____

_____

Evaluate the level of faith in your prayers for family. Are you approaching fervent prayer with unwavering faith, truly believing in God's power to transform challenging family situations?

_____

_____

_____

_____

_____

_____

_____

_____

_____

Reflect on your understanding of prayer's purpose for
families. Do you recognize that it is not about controlling
or manipulating outcomes but about aligning your family
with God's will and seeking His intervention?

_____

_____

_____

_____

_____

_____

_____

Consider your perspective on God's role in your family's life. Are you surrendering family concerns to His care, acknowledging His ultimate authority, and trusting in His wisdom?

_____

_____

Reflect on the impact of prayer on your family bonds. Have you experienced healing, restoration, or protection through prayer? How has prayer influenced your family's unity, communication, forgiveness, and mutual support?

_____

_____

_____

_____

_____

_____

_____

_____

Life-Changing Exercises

1. Take a specific challenge your family is facing and dedicate focused prayer sessions to it. Address the needs, concerns, and desires related to this challenge, seeking God's intervention with specificity.

2. Commit to consistent prayer for your family members. Establish a daily or weekly prayer routine, creating a spiritual force field around your family for ongoing protection and guidance.

3. Initiate a prayer group with other believers who share concerns for their families. Join together in praying for each other's families, amplifying the impact of your prayers through unity and common purpose.

4. Choose a challenging aspect within your family and embark on a faith-building exercise. Regularly pray with unwavering faith and perseverance, trusting in God's transformative power for that specific situation.

Your Past

Chapter Summary

The author emphasizes that while the past cannot be undone, it does not have to define one's identity or limit their potential. Through prayerful confrontation and reliance on God's grace, individuals can find healing, forgiveness, and liberation from the burdens of their past.

This chapter begins by acknowledging the universality of past experiences, from childhood traumas and personal failures to regrets and unresolved conflicts. These experiences can leave emotional scars, hinder spiritual growth, and perpetuate patterns of behavior that hinder personal fulfillment.

The author argues that leaving the past unresolved can lead to a life lived in fear, guilt, and self-doubt. These negative emotions can hinder one's ability to form healthy relationships, pursue their passions, and experience true joy.

In contrast, she presents fervent prayer as a transformative force that can bring healing, forgiveness, and liberation from the past. Through prayer, individuals can:

Acknowledge and confront the past: Prayer creates a safe space for honest introspection and acknowledgment of past hurts and mistakes.

Seek God's forgiveness and healing: Confessing past sins and seeking God's forgiveness allows individuals to experience the cleansing power of grace and release from the burdens of guilt.

Break free from negative patterns: Prayer can help individuals identify and break free from destructive patterns of behavior rooted in past experiences.

Experience restoration and new beginnings: Prayer opens the door to God's restoration, allowing individuals to move forward with a renewed sense of hope and purpose.

She emphasizes that confronting the past through prayer is not about dwelling on past hurts or reliving painful experiences. Instead, it is about acknowledging the impact of the past, seeking God's intervention, and embracing the transformative power of His grace.

Key Lessons

Acknowledging and Confronting the Past is Essential for Healing: While the past cannot be undone, it does not have to define one's identity or limit their potential. Fervent prayer provides a safe space for honest introspection and acknowledgment of past hurts and mistakes.

Seeking God's Forgiveness and Healing is Crucial for Liberation: Prayer allows individuals to confess past sins and seek God's forgiveness, experiencing the cleansing power of grace and release from the burdens of guilt and shame.

Breaking Free from Negative Patterns Requires Intentionality and Prayer: Prayer can help individuals identify and break free from destructive patterns of behavior rooted in past experiences, fostering personal growth and transformation.

Experiencing Restoration and New Beginnings is Possible Through Fervent Prayer: Prayer opens the door to God's restoration, allowing individuals to move forward with a renewed sense of hope, purpose, and freedom from the limitations of the past.

Surrendering Control and Trusting God's Timing is Essential for True Healing: Fervent prayer involves surrendering control of the past to God, trusting His timing for healing and restoration, and embracing His transformative power in one's life.

Self-reflection questions

How can you create a safe space for honest introspection and acknowledgment of your past hurts and mistakes through prayer?

_____

_____

_____

_____

_____

_____

_____

In what ways can confessing your past sins and seeking God's forgiveness contribute to experiencing the cleansing power of grace and release from burdens of guilt?

_____

_____

_____

_____

_____

_____

_____

How might prayer help you identify and break free from destructive patterns of behavior rooted in your past experiences?

_____

_____

_____

_____

_____

_____

_____

_____

What steps can you take through prayer to open the door to God's restoration, allowing you to move forward with a renewed sense of hope and purpose?

_____

_____

_____

_____

_____

_____

_____

_____

_____

How can you differentiate between confronting the past
through prayer for healing and dwelling on past hurts or
reliving painful experiences?

_____

_____

_____

_____

_____

_____

_____

In what specific areas of your life do you recognize the influence of unresolved past experiences, hindering your ability to form healthy relationships, pursue passions, or experience true joy?

_____

_____

_____

_____

_____

_____

_____

Life-Changing Exercises

1. Compile a list of specific past sins or mistakes that weigh on your conscience. Engage in a sincere prayer session to confess these, seeking

God's forgiveness and allowing the cleansing power of grace to alleviate the burdens of guilt.

2. Identify one negative pattern of behavior rooted in past experiences. Through intentional prayer, outline practical steps to break free from this pattern, fostering personal growth and fulfillment.

3. Establish a weekly prayer routine focusing on restoration and new beginnings. Visualize your life with a renewed sense of hope and purpose, and use this time to connect with God's guidance for your journey forward.

4. Attend a group prayer session or join a community focused on spiritual growth. Share your experiences of confronting the past through prayer, and listen to others' stories. This communal practice can deepen your understanding and provide additional support in your transformative journey.

Your Fears

Chapter Summary

In this chapter, the author emphasizes that fear is not a sign of weakness but a common human emotion that can be harnessed or overcome through faith and reliance on God's power.

She begins by acknowledging the universality of fear, recognizing that individuals face a multitude of fears, from fear of failure and rejection to fear of the unknown and the future. These fears can hinder personal growth, limit opportunities, and prevent individuals from living fulfilling lives.

She explains that fear often stems from a lack of trust in God's protection and provision. When individuals place their trust in external factors or seek validation from others, they become vulnerable to the paralyzing effects of fear.

In contrast, the author presents fervent prayer as a powerful weapon against fear, emphasizing its ability to:

Identify and confront the root of fears: Prayer creates a safe space for honest introspection, allowing individuals to uncover the underlying causes of their fears.

Seek God's protection and courage: Prayer invites God's intervention, providing a sense of security and the courage to face challenges head-on.

Replace fear with faith and trust: Prayer fosters a deeper connection with God, replacing fear with trust in His love, guidance, and unwavering presence.

Experience freedom from fear's grip: Prayer can liberate individuals from the shackles of fear, allowing them to live with confidence and pursue their dreams without fear of failure or rejection.

She emphasizes that conquering fear through prayer is not about eliminating fear altogether but about learning to manage it effectively and prevent it from controlling one's life. It is about recognizing that God is greater than any fear and that His love and protection far surpass any perceived threat.

To cultivate fervent prayer for conquering fear, she suggests several practical steps:

1. Identifying specific fears: Reflecting on specific fears or anxieties provides a starting point for focused prayer.

2. Praying for God's intervention: Confessing fears to God and seeking His protection and guidance can bring a sense of peace and reassurance.

3. Replacing fear-based thoughts with God's promises: Prayer can help individuals challenge negative thought patterns and replace them with affirmations rooted in God's word.

4. Surrendering control and trusting God's sovereignty: Fervent prayer involves surrendering control to God and trusting His wisdom and plan, even in the face of fear and uncertainty.

Key Lessons

Fear is a Common Human Emotion but Can Be Overcome Through Fervent Prayer: Fear is not a sign of weakness but a common human emotion that can be harnessed or overcome through faith and reliance on God's power.

Identifying and Confronting the Root of Fears is Essential for Overcoming Them: Prayer creates a safe space for honest introspection, allowing individuals to uncover the underlying causes of their fears, empowering them to address them directly.

Seeking God's Protection and Courage Through Prayer Provides Strength and Reassurance: Prayer invites God's intervention, providing a sense of security, courage, and the strength to face challenges head-on.

Replacing Fear with Faith and Trust Through Prayer Fosters a Deeper Connection with God: Prayer fosters a deeper connection with God, replacing fear with trust in His love, guidance, and unwavering presence, enabling individuals to confront their fears with newfound confidence.

Surrendering Control and Trusting God's Sovereignty Through Prayer Leads to True Freedom from Fear: Fervent prayer involves surrendering control to God, trusting His wisdom and plan, even in the face of fear and uncertainty, leading to true freedom from fear's grip.

Self-reflection questions

Have you acknowledged the universality of fear in your life, recognizing the various fears you face, such as fear of failure, rejection, or the unknown?

_____

_____

_____

_____

_____

_____

_____

In your honest introspection through prayer, have you identified the root causes of your fears, understanding where they stem from and how they impact your life?

_____

_____

_____

_____

_____

Are you placing your trust in external factors or seeking validation from others, making yourself vulnerable to the paralyzing effects of fear, as explained by the author?

In your prayer life, do you actively seek God's protection and courage, inviting His intervention to provide a sense of security and the strength to face challenges head-on?

_____

_____

_____

_____

_____

_____

Are you using prayer to foster a deeper connection with God, replacing fear with trust in His love, guidance, and unwavering presence?

_____

_____

_____

_____

_____

_____

Have you experienced the liberating power of prayer, allowing it to free you from the shackles of fear and enabling you to live with confidence and pursue your dreams without fear of failure or rejection?

_____

_____

_____

_____

_____

_____

In cultivating fervent prayer for conquering fear, are you taking practical steps such as identifying specific fears, confessing them to God, challenging negative thought patterns, and surrendering control to trust in God's sovereignty?

Life-Changing Exercises

1. Create a prayer journal where you confess your fears to God. Regularly write down your anxieties, seeking God's intervention, protection, and guidance. This practice can bring a profound sense of peace and reassurance.

2. Affirmation Replacement Challenge: Identify fear-based thoughts that recurrently occupy your mind. With the power of prayer, challenge and replace these negative thought patterns with affirmations rooted in God's promises. Monitor your progress in shifting your mindset.

3. Choose a day to consciously live without succumbing to fear. Throughout the day, actively engage in fervent prayer whenever fear surfaces. Experience the freedom from fear's grip as you rely on prayer to navigate challenges with courage and trust.

4. Develop a ritual for surrendering control to God's sovereignty. This could involve a specific prayer or meditative practice where you consciously release your fears, trusting in God's wisdom and plan. Regularly incorporate this ritual, especially in moments of fear and uncertainty.

Your Purity

Chapter Summary

This section delves into the importance of purity in a woman's life, highlighting the power of fervent prayer to cultivate inner strength, resist temptation, and experience true fulfillment in one's relationship with God. It mphasizes that purity is not about external perfection but about aligning one's heart and mind with God's standard of holiness, seeking His guidance and empowerment to live a life that honors Him.

The author begins by acknowledging the societal pressures and temptations that women face in today's world, from unrealistic beauty standards to the constant barrage of sexualized messages. These pressures can blur the lines between purity and compromise, leading to confusion and shame.

She explains that true purity extends beyond physical actions and encompasses the thoughts, words, and intentions of the heart. It is about living a life that reflects God's holiness and aligning oneself with His values.

She presents fervent prayer as a transformative force that can cultivate purity in a woman's life, emphasizing its ability to:

Seek God's guidance and wisdom: Prayer invites God's intervention, providing clarity and direction in making choices that align with His standards of purity.

Develop inner strength and resilience: Prayer strengthens a woman's resolve to resist temptation and overcome the pull of sin, fostering self-discipline and moral courage.

Experience God's forgiveness and restoration: Prayer allows individuals to confess wrongdoings and seek God's forgiveness, leading to a renewed sense of purity and a restored relationship with God.

Embrace a life of integrity and purpose: Prayer cultivates a deeper commitment to purity, enabling women to live a life of integrity that reflects God's character and brings true fulfillment.

This chapter emphasizes that the pursuit of purity is not a solo endeavor but a journey undertaken with God's guidance and support. It is about recognizing His love and accepting His grace in the process of transformation.

To cultivate fervent prayer for purity, the author suggests several practical steps:

1. Identifying areas of temptation and vulnerability: Reflecting on specific areas where temptation arises can help formulate focused prayers for strength and protection.

2. Praying for God's protection and empowerment: Confessing temptations and seeking God's intervention can provide a shield against sin and the strength to make wise choices.

3. Seeking guidance from spiritual leaders and mentors: Consultations with trusted spiritual leaders can provide valuable insights, encouragement, and support in the pursuit of purity.

Filling the mind with God's word and positive influences: Enriching one's thoughts with Scripture, uplifting music, and wholesome media can help counteract negative influences and cultivate a mindset that supports purity.

Key Lessons

Purity Extends Beyond Physical Actions and Encompasses Heart, Mind, and Intentions: True purity is not merely about external actions but about aligning one's heart, mind, and intentions with God's standard of holiness, reflecting His character in all aspects of life.

Fervent Prayer Provides Guidance, Wisdom, and Strength to Cultivate Purity: Prayer invites God's intervention, providing clarity, direction, and inner strength to make choices that align with His standards of purity, empowering women to resist temptation and overcome the pull of sin.

Seeking God's Forgiveness and Restoration Promotes True Purity and Renewal: Prayer allows individuals to confess wrongdoings and seek God's forgiveness, leading to a deeper sense of purity, a restored relationship with God, and a renewed commitment to living a life that honors Him.

Embracing a Life of Integrity and Purpose Through Purity Leads to True Fulfillment: Pursuing purity is not about achieving external perfection but about living a life of integrity that reflects God's character and values. This pursuit brings true fulfillment, inner peace, and a deeper connection with God.

Fervent Prayer is a Journey Undertaken with God's Guidance and Support: The pursuit of purity is not a solo endeavor but a collaborative journey undertaken with God's guidance and support. It is about recognizing His love, accepting His grace, and relying on His power for transformation throughout the process.

Self-reflection questions

Have you taken time to reflect on specific areas where temptation arises in your life, understanding the potential vulnerabilities that may lead to compromising situations?

In your prayer life, are you consistently seeking God's guidance and wisdom, inviting His intervention to provide clarity and direction in the choices you make regarding purity?

_____

_____

_____

_____

_____

_____

Through prayer, have you actively worked on developing inner strength and resilience, strengthening your resolve to resist temptation and fostering self-discipline and moral courage?

_____

_____

_____

_____

_____

_____

_____

Are you utilizing prayer to confess wrongdoings, seek God's forgiveness, and experience the renewal of purity and restoration in your relationship with Him?

_____

_____

_____

_____

_____

Is your commitment to purity extending beyond external actions to encompass your thoughts, words, and intentions of the heart? How is prayer helping you live a life that reflects God's holiness and values?

_____

_____

_____

_____

_____

_____

_____

_____

Do you recognize that the pursuit of purity is a journey undertaken with God's guidance and support? How are you acknowledging His love and accepting His grace in the process of transformation?

_____

_____

_____

_____

_____

_____

_____

Life-Changing Exercises

1. Take time to identify specific areas of your life where temptation tends to arise. Create a personal "Temptation Terrain Map" to guide your prayers

for strength and protection in these vulnerable areas.

2. Integrate a daily protection prayer routine into your life. Consistently confess temptations to God and seek His intervention for empowerment, building a shield against sin and fortifying your ability to make wise choices.

3. Initiate or strengthen connections with spiritual leaders and mentors. Engage in conversations that provide insights, encouragement, and support in your pursuit of purity, recognizing the value of shared wisdom in your journey.

4. Establish a routine of filling your mind with God's word. Incorporate Scripture reading and reflection into your daily life, using it as a powerful tool to counteract negative influences and cultivate a mindset aligned with purity.

Your Pressures

Chapter Summary

This section details the multitude of pressures women face in today's society, highlighting the power of fervent prayer to bring relief, clarity, and a renewed sense of purpose amidst overwhelming demands. It outline the fact that while pressures are inevitable, they do not have to define one's identity or control one's life. Through prayerful surrender and reliance on God's strength, women can navigate life's challenges with grace, resilience, and unwavering faith.

The author begins by acknowledging the diverse pressures women face, from societal expectations and familial obligations to the pursuit of personal goals and career aspirations. These pressures can lead to feelings of inadequacy, anxiety, and burnout, hindering personal fulfillment and making it difficult to prioritize one's well-being.

She explains that pressures often stem from the desire to meet external expectations and achieve societal standards. This pursuit of external validation can leave women feeling overwhelmed and disconnected from their true selves and their relationship with God.

In contrast, she presents fervent prayer as a powerful tool for managing pressures and finding peace amidst life's demands. Prayer can help women:

Identify and acknowledge the root causes of pressure: Prayer creates a safe space for honest introspection, allowing women to uncover the underlying sources of stress and anxiety.

Seek God's guidance and perspective: Prayer invites God's intervention, providing clarity and a fresh perspective on life's challenges, helping women prioritize and make decisions based on their values and God's guidance.

Receive strength and resilience: Prayer empowers women with God's strength to face challenges, overcome obstacles, and navigate difficult situations with grace and resilience.

Surrender control and trust in God's timing: Fervent prayer involves surrendering control to God, trusting His plan and timing, even in the face of uncertainty and pressure.

The author emphasizes that prayer is not a means of escaping pressures but a tool for managing them effectively and preventing them from controlling one's life. It is about recognizing God's sovereignty, trusting His love, and seeking His wisdom in navigating life's challenges.

Key Lessons

Pressures Are Inevitable but Do Not Have to Define or Control One's Life: While pressures are a common part of life, they do not have to define one's identity or dictate one's choices. Fervent prayer can help women recognize their true worth and navigate life's challenges with grace and resilience.

Identifying and Acknowledging the Root Causes of Pressure is Essential for Effective Management: Prayer creates a safe space for honest introspection, allowing women to uncover the underlying sources of stress and anxiety, enabling them to address the root causes rather than merely reacting to the symptoms.

Seeking God's Guidance and Perspective Provides Clarity and Direction: Prayer invites God's intervention, providing a fresh perspective on life's challenges and helping women make decisions aligned with their values and God's purpose, leading to a more fulfilling and purposeful life.

Receiving Strength and Resilience Through Prayer Empowers Women to Overcome Obstacles: Fervent prayer empowers women with God's strength to face challenges, overcome obstacles, and navigate difficult situations with grace and resilience, enabling them to persevere and achieve their goals.

Surrendering Control and Trusting in God's Timing Brings Peace and Serenity Amidst Pressures: Fervent prayer involves surrendering control to God, trusting His plan and timing, even in the face of uncertainty and pressure, leading to a deeper sense of peace, trust, and inner strength.

Self-reflection questions

Have you taken the time to prayerfully reflect on the specific sources of pressure in your life, uncovering the roots of stress and anxiety that may be affecting your well-being?

_____

_____

_____

_____

_____

_____

_____

_____

In your prayer life, are you consistently seeking God's guidance and perspective on the challenges you face, allowing His intervention to provide clarity and a fresh outlook to help you prioritize and make decisions aligned with your values?

_____

_____

_____

_____

_____

_____

Through prayer, have you actively sought God's strength to face challenges, overcome obstacles, and navigate difficult situations with grace and resilience? How has this strengthened your ability to cope with life's demands?

_____

_____

_____

_____

_____

_____

_____

Are you practicing the art of surrender in your prayers, letting go of the need to control every aspect of your life and trusting in God's plan and timing, especially in moments of uncertainty and pressure?

_____

How are you using prayer as a tool for managing pressures effectively, preventing them from controlling your life? Reflect on instances where prayer has been instrumental in bringing relief and peace amidst overwhelming demands.

_____

_____

_____

_____

_____

_____

In the pursuit of meeting external expectations, do you find yourself feeling disconnected from your true self and your relationship with God? How can prayer help you realign with your authentic identity and strengthen your connection with God?

_____

_____

_____

_____

_____

_____

_____

_____

Consider your approach to decision-making. Are you integrating prayer as a means to seek God's wisdom before making choices, ensuring that your decisions are in alignment with your values and guided by His perspective?

_____

_____

_____

_____

_____

_____

Life-Changing Exercises

1. Create a "Root Causes Journal" where you regularly engage in prayerful introspection to identify and acknowledge the underlying sources of stress and anxiety in your life. This practice can bring clarity and pave the way for targeted prayer.

2. Dedicate specific prayer sessions to seek God's guidance and perspective on the challenges you're facing. Allow these moments to bring clarity and a fresh outlook, helping you prioritize and make decisions aligned with your values and God's guidance.

3. Integrate strength and resilience affirmations into your daily prayer routine. Use these affirmations to actively receive God's strength, empowering you to face challenges, overcome obstacles, and navigate difficult situations with grace.

4. Establish a routine where you prayerfully prioritize your well-being. During these moments of reflection, seek God's wisdom in understanding how to balance societal expectations, familial obligations, and personal goals, ensuring that your decisions align with His guidance and bring peace to your life.

Your Hearts

Chapter Summary

In this chapter, the author acknowledges the vulnerabilities of the heart, recognizing that it is susceptible to external influences, temptations, and negative thoughts that can lead to spiritual compromise and emotional turmoil. She emphasizes that guarding one's heart is not about creating a fortress of isolation but about cultivating a sanctuary of purity, love, and joy, aligned with God's will.

In contrast, the chapter presents fervent prayer as a powerful shield for the heart, emphasizing its ability to:

Seek God's protection and cleansing: Prayer invites God's intervention, providing a protective shield against negative influences and seeking His cleansing power to remove impure thoughts and emotions.

Cultivate purity of mind and heart: Prayer fosters a deeper connection with God, aligning one's thoughts and emotions with His standards of purity, leading to a life of integrity and moral clarity.

Experience true joy and fulfillment: Prayer opens the door to God's overflowing joy and peace, filling the heart with contentment and a sense of purpose, leading to a life of fulfillment and satisfaction.

Discern between God's voice and worldly distractions: Prayer enhances the ability to discern between God's gentle guidance and the distractions and temptations of the world, fostering wisdom and clarity in making decisions.

The author emphasizes that guarding one's heart through fervent prayer is an ongoing process, requiring consistent communication with God and a willingness to surrender control over one's inner world. It is about recognizing God as the source of true protection, purity, and joy.

Key Lessons

The Heart is a Battleground for Spiritual Forces, and Fervent Prayer is a Vital Weapon: The heart, as the seat of emotions, desires, and intentions, is susceptible to external influences and temptations. Fervent prayer acts as a shield, protecting the heart from negative influences and fostering purity of mind and emotion.

Guarding the Heart is Not About Isolation but Cultivating a Sanctuary of Purity, Love, and Joy: Guarding the heart through fervent prayer is not about creating a fortress of isolation but about cultivating a sanctuary aligned with God's will. It is about seeking His protection and cleansing power to remove impure thoughts and emotions, allowing true joy and fulfillment to flourish.

Fervent Prayer Enhances the Ability to Discern God's Voice Amidst Worldly Distractions: Prayer fosters a deeper connection with God, enabling one to distinguish between His gentle guidance and the distractions and temptations of the world. This discernment leads to wisdom and clarity in decision-making, aligning one's actions with God's purpose.

Guarding the Heart Through Fervent Prayer is an Ongoing Process Requiring Consistent Communication with God and Surrender of Control: Protecting the heart is an ongoing journey, requiring consistent prayer and a willingness to surrender control over one's inner world to God's guidance and protection. It is about recognizing God as the source of true purity, joy, and lasting fulfillment.

Self-reflection questions

Have you taken the time to honestly assess the vulnerabilities of your heart, considering external influences, temptations, and negative thoughts that might be impacting your spiritual well-being?

_____

_____

_____

_____

_____

In your prayer life, do you actively seek God's protection for your heart? How is prayer serving as a protective shield against negative influences, and how are you inviting God's cleansing power to remove impure thoughts and emotions?

_____

_____

_____

_____

_____

_____

_____

_____

_____

Through prayer, are you fostering a deeper connection with God, aligning your thoughts and emotions with His standards of purity? Reflect on how prayer is contributing to a life of integrity and moral clarity.

_____

_____

_____

_____

_____

_____

_____

_____

_____

_____

Examine the role of prayer in your life. How has prayer opened the door to God's joy and peace, contributing to a sense of contentment and purpose? Reflect on moments where prayer has led to true fulfillment.

_____

_____

_____

_____

_____

_____

_____

Consider your ability to discern between God's voice and worldly distractions. How has prayer enhanced your discernment, fostering wisdom and clarity in decision-making? Reflect on instances where prayer played a role in navigating distractions and temptations.

_____

_____

_____

_____

_____

_____

_____

_____

Life-Changing Exercises

1. Create intentional joyful prayer moments throughout your day. These brief pauses can be moments of gratitude, where you express thanks to God. Use these moments to invite God's overflowing joy and peace into your heart, fostering contentment and a sense of purpose.

2. Set aside a day for a distraction-free prayer retreat. Disconnect from worldly distractions and spend dedicated time in fervent prayer. Focus on enhancing your discernment between God's voice and worldly temptations, seeking wisdom and clarity for decisions you face.

3. Develop a nightly "Heart Surrender Ritual" where you consciously surrender control over your inner world to God. Through prayer, release any burdens, impure thoughts, or emotions. Embrace this as a consistent practice in recognizing God as the ongoing source of true protection, purity, and joy in your life

Your Relationships

Chapter Summary

The author delves into the complexities of human relationships, highlighting the power of fervent prayer to cultivate healing, forgiveness, and lasting connections. She emphasizes that relationships, while a source of great joy and fulfillment, can also be a source of conflict, hurt, and disappointment. Fervent prayer provides a transformative tool to navigate the challenges of relationships, fostering empathy, understanding, and the ability to love unconditionally.

This section begins by acknowledging the universality of relational struggles, from familial tensions and friendships gone astray to navigating the complexities of romantic relationships. These struggles can leave individuals feeling isolated, misunderstood, and burdened by unresolved issues.

She explains that relational challenges often stem from unmet expectations, unresolved conflicts, or communication breakdowns. These issues can fester, leading to resentment, bitterness, and the erosion of trust.

Key Lessons

Relationships, While a Source of Joy and Fulfillment, Can Also Be a Source of Conflict and Disappointment: Fervent prayer provides a transformative tool to navigate the challenges of relationships, fostering empathy, understanding, and the ability to love unconditionally.

Relational Struggles Often Stem from Unmet Expectations, Unresolved Conflicts, or Communication Breakdowns: Prayer can help individuals identify the root causes of relational conflicts, providing clarity and perspective to address these issues effectively.

Fervent Prayer Cultivates Empathy and Understanding, Enabling Individuals to See Others Through God's Eyes: Prayer fosters a deeper connection with God and others, allowing individuals to extend empathy and compassion, even in the face of differences and imperfections.

Prayer Empowers Individuals to Release Resentment, Forgive Past Hurts, and Seek Reconciliation, Opening the Door to Healing and Renewed Connection: Fervent prayer promotes forgiveness and reconciliation, breaking the chains of bitterness and allowing relationships to heal and grow.

Prayer Fosters a Deeper Understanding of God's Unconditional Love, Enabling Individuals to Love Others with Compassion and Acceptance: Fervent prayer cultivates a spirit of unconditional love, empowering individuals to extend love and acceptance to others, even in the face of flaws and shortcomings.

Self-reflection questions

Have you taken time to reflect on the complexities of your relationships, recognizing the potential sources of conflict, hurt, or disappointment, and acknowledging the universality of relational struggles?

In your introspection, consider the relational challenges you've faced. Have you identified instances where unmet expectations, unresolved conflicts, or breakdowns in communication contributed to struggles? How have these factors affected your relationships?

Reflect on moments when relational challenges left you feeling burdened or isolated. How did these struggles impact your well-being, and in what ways did you cope with the feelings of isolation or misunderstanding?

How has fervent prayer served as a transformative tool in navigating the challenges of your relationships? Reflect on specific instances where prayer facilitated healing, forgiveness, and a deeper understanding in your connections with others.

_____

_____

_____

_____

_____

_____

_____

_____

Consider your ability to love unconditionally in your relationships. How has prayer played a role in fostering empathy and understanding, enabling you to love others despite challenges? Reflect on the impact of prayer in cultivating lasting connections based on love and forgiveness

----

Life-Changing Exercises

1. Integrate a forgiveness meditation into your routine. During this practice, focus on individuals with whom you have unresolved issues. Through

fervent prayer, release feelings of resentment or bitterness, fostering a heart ready for forgiveness and understanding.

2. Initiate empathetic conversations with individuals in your life. Use fervent prayer to guide these interactions, seeking to understand their perspectives and feelings. This practice can strengthen connections and foster a deeper sense of empathy.

3. Develop a trust restoration prayer for relationships where trust has been eroded. Consistently pray for guidance in rebuilding trust, understanding the steps needed for reconciliation, and fostering an environment conducive to rebuilding lasting connections based on love and forgiveness.

Final Evaluation Questions

What did you learn from this workbook that you didn't know before?

_____

_____

_____

_____

_____

_____

How has the information in this workbook impacted your understanding of the subject matter?

_____

_____

_____

_____

Can you identify any areas where you still feel uncertain or would like further clarification?

_____

_____

_____

_____

Describe any challenges you faced while completing the exercises in this workbook and how you overcame them.

_____

_____

_____

_____

How do you plan to apply the knowledge and skills you've gained from this workbook in your work or daily life?

_____

_____

_____

_____

_____

Are there any specific topics or concepts you would like to explore further after completing this workbook?

_____

_____

_____

_____

Overall, how would you rate your learning experience with this workbook on a scale of 1 to 10, with 10 being the highest? Please explain your rating.

_____

_____

Dear reader,

Thank you for choosing this workbook. Your engagement with the content is truly appreciated. As an author, I am committed to continuous improvement and providing valuable insights to my readers.

I kindly request a moment of your time to share your thoughts on the book. Your honest review will not only provide valuable feedback but also assist potential readers in making informed decisions.

Please consider addressing the following points in your review:

What resonated with you the most?
Were the questions and exercises helpful?
How would you describe the overall impact of the book on your understanding or perspective?
Were the chapter summaries effective in reinforcing key concepts?

Your input is instrumental in shaping future projects and ensuring that they meet the expectations of readers like you. Feel free to express your thoughts openly, as your feedback is genuinely valued.

Once again, thank you for your time and consideration. Your support means the world, and I am eager to hear your insights.

Best Regards,
Willow Reads Workbook Team.

Made in the USA
Coppell, TX
24 June 2025